The Booklet of 8s

Krsnanandini Devi Dasi

Prema Press | Cleveland

The Booklet of 8s

Cover by Taraka Goodman-Robinson. Interior illustrations by Hari-Gaura Ziyad. Copy editing and interior layout by Empathik LLC.

Printed in the United States of America.

ISBN 978-0-9882097-0-1

The Booklet of Eights

Table of Contents

Introduction 1

8 Universal Spiritual Laws 3

8 Steps to Self-Discipline 9

8 Principles of Prosperity 13

8 Rules for Effective, Meaningful Discussions 17

8 Signs of a Healthy Male-Female Relationship 21

8 Tips for Successful Parenting 23

8 Qualities of a Spiritual Warrior 27

8 Books to Read to Enhance Your Life 33

Introduction

Recently, the Dasi-Ziyad Family Institute attorney's administrative assistant called to reschedule an appointment. We both laughed as we checked and re-checked our appointment calendars to make sure we weren't over scheduling our already full days. And, we lamented because precious time seemed to elude us.

People are so busy today! Often, we feel we don't have enough time to read books about relationships, spirituality, self-development, or other mentally rejuvenating topics as much as we would like. If we attend a workshop or seminar, frequently time seems to run out before we can fully explore the subject matter. It was after one such workshop in which we facilitated a Healthy Relationship session that one of our staff members implored us to create a series of succinct books that would contain many of the gems we discuss in our workshops and in our conference presentations.

She told us that many people would appreciate such condensed insights because they delve into the essence of who we are and would connect a person to his or her real self even when we keep so externally busy. The gifts found in this *Booklet of 8s* help us to reflect on how to live healthier, more productive and satisfying lives.

Therefore, in these pages, the reader will find seeds that, when thoughtfully planted, will sprout and grow into enhancing insights and realizations about life, parenting, healthy communication, spirituality and more. *The Booklet of 8s* is designed to motivate you to look inwardly, find your humanity and, beyond that, discover your soul.

Each step, each principle or tip is meant to act as a catalyst to get your higher energies flowing and to empower you to keep growing, expanding and connecting. We encourage you to meditate on or study daily at least one of the eight topics discussed in this book.

Take just 8 minutes a day to study one or all of the 8 short chapters with its 8 points. Your ability to understand and find solutions to many of the challenges in your life will increase after you reflect on and unpack these 64 considerations.

8 Universal Spiritual Laws

All of you sons of immortality, hear, you who once resided in the divine kingdom. —Svetasvatara Upanisad 2.5

A spiritual law is a principle that is true in all situations and in all places at all times. It is a universal truth whose authority and implementation is divine, coming from a source higher than man. Just as there are local, state and federal laws, each successively more authoritative, so there are divine or spiritual laws that come from the Supreme Authority, God. Such laws are reliable, irrevocable and eternal. Sometimes man-made laws can become useless, outdated or even illegal.

Not so with divine, spiritual laws. Irrefutable and transcendent, spiritual laws can never be changed, can never become irrelevant or obsolete. By understanding these laws and being in harmony with them, you can find peace and satisfaction wherever you are.

1. The Law of Unity: All life is connected; there is unity in all living things.

We have a common source, the Creator of all. Every life, every spiritual spark, comes from this ONE Creator. What each of us does, what each of thinks, therefore, affects the whole of the universe. Like the spider web affected by the slightest touch, the web of life, or the circle of life, is affected by the touch or actions of each living being. This brings us to the conclusion that "your success is my success." When you

3

help someone to fare well, when you encourage someone, then their growth or their progress helps you. When you make a conscious choice to give of yourself for a greater principle, you benefit the entire world. The opposite is also true. Why? Because we are interconnected! Researchers recently discovered a surprising connection between the elimination of a tiny insect on a remote island, an increase in frogs and the disturbance of the whole ecological balance on the island. Another way to look at this law is the analogy that when you water the root of a tree, the whole tree is benefited.

2.   The Law of Karma: For every action, there is an equal and opposite reaction. In other words, "you reap what you sow."

All the major scriptures of the world reflect this universal principle. No sane person expects to get an apple tree from an orange seed. Similarly we cannot expect to get good results from bad deeds. Those who hurt others, or act out of greed, deception, or false ego will experience negative reactions from these behaviors. Guaranteed. Just as when we plant a seed of a tree and it takes time to develop, reactions take time to manifest. Even if it appears sometimes that people get away with doing hurtful or sinful acts, the Divine Eye always observes, records, and distributes consequences, either immediately or later. As stated in the Bible, "you reap what you sow." Sinful, greedy, lusty or mean-spirited behavior has negative consequences. Good or pious behavior connects us to good results.

3.   The Law of Greatness: Humility and service is the key to greatness.

"He that would be the greatest among you, let him become the servant of all" (Lord Jesus Christ). Or, as the ancient proverb, a paradox, states, "The way up is down." "Everyone can be great because everyone can serve" (Dr. Martin Luther King Jr.). Acting in such a way that we recognize that there is One Supreme Controller, One Master, One Boss and you, like other living beings, are His eternal servant, will allow us to flow in harmony with the Universal Order, the order that gives you the best results. Just consider that there are trillions (unlimited) of living beings in our universe. And there are an unlimited number of universes, each populated with life.

Yet, order in creation is being maintained so that our sun rises and sets every day and so many organic processes take place over which we have no control. You may then come to realize that you are an infinitesimal part of the Infinite. If you think you are the controller, the lord of all you survey, nature has a definite way of bringing you to reality. False pride and arrogance are traps that keep us from truly appreciating that our greatness comes through acknowledging how small we are, how much we don't know in comparison to the Creator of all. Such an attitude of humility coupled with appreciation is the winning key to real greatness.

4. The Law of Rhythm or Vibration: Everything in creation vibrates.

Even solid items are vibrating at very slow rates. Everything is moving, though at greater or lesser speeds. In this universe, change is a constant. Scientists have even identified that the earth itself is constantly expanding. Everything is moving towards achieving balance and harmony. What happens when there is harmony? There is agreement between different things and a healthy stability and order is established. Gradually chaos and confusion disappear as you get in harmony with the divine will. The vibration of people who are God conscious or principled in their behavior is higher than those who engage in unclean, cruel or dishonest activities.

5. The Law of Mortality/Immortality. All matter has a beginning and an end. All spiritual beings are eternal.

Thus, whatever is born must die. The distinction between matter and spirit is extremely important since the nature of matter is that it is temporary; spirit is eternal. As stated in the previous law, material change is inevitable. Only material bodies are born, and material bodies, despite our best efforts or technological advances, must die. This is important because our attachment to material bodies and mundane things can cause great pain.

Realizing that we are spiritual beings having a material experience will help us to focus on priorities. We will focus on developing healthy relationships rather than acquiring more and more things. Instead of devoting all of our energy to caring only for the body, we will care for and feed our soul as well. The spirit soul, the spark of life within each of us, is never born and therefore can never die. To paraphrase the great scientist, Albert Einstein, "Life (Energy) can neither be created nor destroyed."

6. The Law of Existence (sometimes called the Law of Dharma): There is a reality beyond this phenomenal world — beyond the world of the five senses and the five great material elements (earth, water, fire, air and ether) and our purpose is to re-establish our connection to this Reality.

Acknowledging and understanding our spiritual consciousness is where real happiness begins. Seeking confirmation of his existence, the French philosopher Rene Descartes declared, "I think, therefore, I am." This is only partially accurate; the whole truth is that "God thinks, therefore, I (an individual person,) am." You are a thought or expression in the eternal mind of God. Because God is the Absolute Truth, the Absolute Reality, His thoughts are reality. We (all the living beings) live, move and have our existence in God. Happiness and peace comes when we awaken from our illusion of separateness and return to harmony within this Divine Supreme Reality.

7. The Law of Respect and Order: In order to progress steadily, we must respect and honor the authorities and ancestors who cared for us and paved the way for our civilization.

Failure to respect and honor our parents and other authorities causes dire social consequences such as broken families, failure to pass on important cultural and family traditions and neglect of wise, hard-working elders. Each and every human being is the recipient of the grace of persons who have gone before us, creating roads, both physical and spiritual, on which we travel. We are indebted to those who have built schools, roads and hospitals, and made inventions and systems that make our lives more convenient and facilitate our progress. Additionally, we owe much to those great souls who have chalked out spiritual paths and have left their invaluable instructions and their examples for us to follow.

8. The Law of Love: The highest universal spiritual principle is love.

God is love personified. While love can be defined in many ways, we see that one of the clearest definitions of love is "truly wanting the best or the good for others so much so that you are willing to devote yourself and make sacrifices for their best interests." We can't really be happy or healthy without love since loving affection is actually a need of the spirit soul. Unfortunately, we often confuse lust, infatuation and/or emotional needs with love. The secret is not to seek love, but to give or share love unconditionally.

Reflect on these 8 spiritual laws and you will come closer to identifying your purpose in this life. Think about what you'd like to accomplish. How do your goals, attitudes and ideas align with these 8 Universal laws?

8 Steps to Self-Discipline

"Early to bed, early to rise, makes a person healthy, wealthy and wise." — Benjamin Franklin

In order to achieve great, important or necessary things over a period of time, maintaining a structure or framework to fulfill your goals and keep you disciplined is a vital step along your spiritual path. You cannot contribute to others' lives without first committing to your own progress. Each of the following steps will assist you in improving your life. Unless you exercise self-control, most significant accomplishments will elude you. So the choice is up to you. Try implementing these 8 steps to gain discipline in your life and see the difference.

1.   Declare your intentions by setting specific goals; ask yourself why you want to change your own behavior.

A client, we will call her Cheryl, called recently, concerned that she was about to lose her marriage. She was depressed and overwhelmed and realized that she had wrapped her happiness completely in one man and was losing her sense of self. She decided that she wanted to work to find her spiritual center, her own equilibrium, so that even if she lost her husband, she would not lose herself. She began to follow a schedule that included prayer and meditation. She declared her intention to set aside time for internal reflection no matter what happened.

2. Seek advice and guidance from elders or experienced family, friends or spiritual leaders.

A minister she respected told Cheryl to read the Bible, Qur'an, Bhagavad-gita — any one of the bonafide holy books — and select one verse a day from her chosen scripture to meditate on a regular basis. He suggested this to help Cheryl focus and tune in to her Higher Power (inner spiritual power of God), the source of real strength.

3. Set realistic, attainable and simple (at first) goals.

You will feel empowered and motivated when you achieve your goals. At the same time, your goals should involve some challenge, some stretching of your mental and physical abilities. So, set realistic and attainable goals, and then challenge yourself to do more. After Cheryl assessed her time, energy and aspirations, she concluded that she would actually be able to achieve the goal she set.

4. Establish definite, specific routines for taking rest, taking meals, doing chores, studying or meditating, working out, and spending time with your children.

For example, Cheryl chose to meditate once a day for five minutes in the morning before work or school. She started with five minutes and gradually, over a period of 8 weeks, she increased her meditation to 15 minutes daily.

5. Decide what you will do if you break your self-imposed rule.

Cheryl decided that if she missed her mediation in the morning, "I will do it at night before I go to sleep."

6. Pray daily for the spiritual strength to keep your word to yourself!

Those who are conscious understand that making vows and keeping them is an important commitment that strengthens you internally.

Be persistent. Even if you forget once or twice, continue with your routine. Don't be discouraged. Remember this goal is something you really want to accomplish. When you pray for help, you are asking for divine help from a power much greater than you and your sincere prayer and actions will help with your resolve.

7. Reward yourself for following through.

Cheryl's reward to herself was: "Once I've meditated for a month, I'll treat myself to a delicious meal at my favorite vegetarian restaurant."

8. Periodically review your progress and make adjustments when you need to.

At the end of each week, analyze how this meditation is affecting you. Are you more patient or peaceful? Are you able to concentrate?

8 Principles of Prosperity

"O Lord, The earth is full of your riches." —Psalms 104: 24,
(Bible, King James Version)

Prosperity, I am sure you will agree, is not about having lots of money. It is a state of consciousness in which our lives are enriched. We feel fulfilled and are content with what we have while we are assured that what is meant for us will come to us. We work with a healthy, enlivening sense of well-being. A prosperous person is always aware of being connected to the source of everything. In this source, there is no lack or limitation. Thus, these principles of prosperity are inspired by the realizations of the Universal Laws delineated in the previous chapter.

1. Recognize God, the Supreme Owner.

Act with the understanding that everything belongs to God. He is the Source of all life, the Cause of all causes. At best, you are a careful steward of God's resources, energies and talents. At worst, you are a thief, claiming God's property as your own.

2. Use God's resources in careful stewardship.

Prosperous people consciously perform their duties taking care of self, family and community as an act of worship. Realize you've been entrusted with family, talents and wealth that are really not your own. Prosperous people "plan their work and work their plan" through budgeting, keeping good financial records and creating a vision of their prosperity through goal setting.

3. Be mindful of your spending habits.

"Waste not, want not." Consider that everything you waste has consequences of producing scarcity. Sometimes just a little thoughtfulness will prevent great waste. Those who are truly thrifty will thrive. Especially in western countries, much food is wasted and often tools and machines that break down are junked instead of being repaired. The scriptures and wise, saintly people tell us that there is no waste in the eternal spiritual world. Therefore, increasing prosperity means reducing waste.

4. Give and you may receive.

This is perhaps the most misunderstood principle of prosperity. Tithing or contributing to charities, good causes or helping others, creates not only monetary abundance, but also spiritual wealth. This tithing is an investment in the divine bank of the Universe. When you give of yourself, your time, your money or other resources to uplifting, empowering or spiritual causes, you reap powerful rewards. Sometimes when we feel scarcity, we tend to give less freely when actually, this is the time to give more, despite appearances. Donating money is only a piece of the gift-giving puzzle. Contributing your time and support to worthy projects, people and events is extremely important.

5. Live a regulated, disciplined life.

By leading a productive and regulated life, you can focus your energies on what's most important. "One who can control his senses by practicing the regulated principles of freedom can obtain the complete mercy of the Lord and thus become free from all attachment and aversion." (Bhagavad-gita 2:64). Setting scheduled, regular times for prayer, family and time to yourself will help you keep centered. Going to bed at a reasonable time and rising early, even if you nap during the day, will help keep you at your best.

6. Share your success with others.

The prosperity mentality, the winner mentality, is one in which you are an example for another. "What you give away is also what you get to keep." Teach someone how to do what you have done. Share the benefit of your successful techniques and skills with others. Become a mentor.

7. Live simply but think highly.

Adopt a simple lifestyle. Begin by carefully analyzing your choices in eating, behavior and purchases. Do you really need all of the stuff that you spend so much time accumulating? Keep your living space free of clutter. (This may be a constant challenge in the western culture where consumerism is the name of the game; where both planned and perceived obsolescence causes people to get rid of still usable items and purchase newer and newer ones; where manufacturers distribute goods that they know have shorter duration than necessary; and where advertisers and marketers make people think that yesterday's shoes, clothes, household items, even though still in good shape, are no longer stylish or usable today.) Choose to think deeply, spiritually and live an uncomplicated, uncluttered and unpretentious life.

8. Cultivate a prosperity consciousness.

Many people, even those with some material assets, have a "poverty consciousness." This is a sense of lack or scarcity, or the idea that you do not have enough of what you need and that you will likely never have enough of what you need. It implies fear, anxiety or paranoia about having sufficient resources to survive or flourish.

Realize that God, your Creator, your best well-wisher and your dearest friend, wants you to prosper. It is directly God's divine will that you have abundant health and the capability to care for yourself and fulfill your responsibilities.

Prosperity is truly a state of consciousness. If you utilize these 8 principles in your daily life, the prosperous consciousness is yours without a doubt. When you practice the principles consistently and regularly, without neglecting any, it will help you avoid poverty consciousness.

8 Rules for Effective, Meaningful Discussions

"The character of a man is known from his conversations"
—Menander (342 BC - 292 BC)

Sharing yourself with others is one of the greatest gifts you can give. The real treasure in human relationships, however, is the ability to listen respectfully and carefully and participate in conversations where you understand and are understood.

Generally, people speak because they want to share, get answers, connect or heal themselves. In order to be effective in your communication, listen to yourself and others with an open heart and soul. Leslie, another client, shared a room with a college friend during her junior and senior years. They remained friends for decades. Says Leslie, "She is the best listener and I really try to hear what she says too. It's so reassuring to have someone who listens without judgment."

1. **Listen well.** Use reflective listening and summarize what others say to you. Try to understand and be considerate and respectful of the other person's view. (Believe it or not, the best speakers are the best listeners — and readers.) "Because I heard nicely, I could speak nicely." —Bhaktivedanta Swami, Vedic saint and philosopher.

2. **Allow each other to communicate without interruptions.** Listen with earnest intention and try to maintain a quiet mind so you clearly hear what the other is

saying, instead of anxiously formulating your response or rebuttal. Remember, your goal is to hear the needs of the other.

3. Use kind, thoughtful words that are centered on building one another up. Two things are important in this regard: Your words can be builders or destroyers. And, scientists tell us that about 80% of communication is non-verbal. So allow your body and your facial expressions to purposely communicate how you feel or what you think. Sit or stand in a relaxed fashion with your arms at your side. Gentle facial expressions will make the other person feel at ease. In other words, you communicate with your words, your body and your facial expressions.

4. Honor and respect confidences. Sharing feelings, needs and desires creates a connection between people, but we also become vulnerable, exposing our emotions, hurts and sensitivities. Keep what is said between you and others to yourself (except by permission or emergency).

5. Know when to quit. Discussion can sometimes become elevated with intense emotion and anxiety. Call a time-out if the discussion escalates to the point where you are too angry, become too distracted or cannot speak respectfully. Then, agree to a definite time to continue the discussion.

6. Share the moments. Providing enough time for each other to speak will keep the flow of conversation active and interesting. Respect one another's communication styles. You may be very vocal and articulate while your friend, spouse or employee may be quieter, introverted or more deliberate in speech. Nonetheless, slow down enough to listen to him or her.

7. Think before you speak. Words, once uttered, cannot be erased. Consider what you say, where you say it and to whom you are saying it. Be considerate of the time, place and circumstances of any conversation in which you participate. Weigh your words carefully and ask yourself: Is what you are saying *true*? Is it *necessary*? And, is it *kind* (or helpful to the discussion)?

8. Speak truthfully, that is — honestly. Deceit and dishonesty destroy trust or respect and indicate a cheating mentality. Deceit, dishonesty and cheating are some seeds for creating poverty. Truth is the groundwork for freedom. "You shall know the truth and the truth shall make you free" (Bible).

8 Signs of a Healthy Male-Female Relationship

"Intimate relationships cannot substitute for a life plan. But to have any meaning or viability at all, a life plan must include intimate relationships." —Harriet Lerner

Healthy relationships are likely the most essential element to the well-being of individuals, families and communities. Relationships, particularly between male and female, are filled with challenges in today's fast, often impersonal world. The good news is that there are skills you can learn and commitments you can make to have healthy, satisfying relationships. The following are signs of energizing and reciprocal relationships:

1. You accept a common spirituality where you recognize God and the existence of Divine principles. This spirituality is the basis for your behavior and your decision-making.

2. You have a support system consisting of your community, friends and family; this support system is accessible and utilized by both of you. "Treasure your relationships, not your possessions." (A.J. D'Angelo)

3. You can and do openly communicate with each other about individual, couple and family concerns. Consideration, respect, honesty, and appreciation characterize your communication. Both of you avoid discussing heavy issues in public. You honor confidence within your relationship and avoid backbiting. When talking to one another, you generally use thoughtful and caring words, rather than cursing, putting down or condemning.

4. You create a financial plan, including budgeting and saving together. Openly discussing debts, income protection and financial growth is a very important part of a healthy marriage/relationship and one that couples often neglect.

5. You make time to be together regularly and you allow each other to have personal space as well. Healthy couples are not intimidated when one has separate time or space. They do not feel threatened.

6. You view yourself as a unit, team members working to accomplish common goals. You develop goals for yourself, each other and your family.

7. You agree on a system for disciplining and raising your children and/or dealing with close family members and friends.

8. You are open to seeking help or enrichment to improve your marital/relationship skills (communication, conflict resolution, financial planning, goal setting, spirituality). You actively seek workshops, books and other resources to enhance your relationship.

Test yourself. Can you say that you and your partner have a healthy relationship by being affirmative in all or most of these signs?

8 Tips for Successful Parenting

"Train up a child in the way he should go; and when he is old he will not depart from it." — Proverbs 22:6 (Bible, King James Version)

Parenting is such a serious responsibility! It is an art and a commitment that begs careful, steady cultivation. In fact, the ancient Vedas (a large body of scriptures originating in ancient India and recorded in the ancient Sanskrit language, the Vedas mean "knowledge" and are the oldest sacred, spiritual texts of Hinduism) state that one should not become a mother or father unless she or he is able to revive the dormant spiritual consciousness of their child(ren). By the same token, these scriptures do not advocate abortion or artificial birth control.

Biblical scriptures also say that we should "train a child in the way that he or she should go, and when the child is older, the training will not depart from the child." Thus, parents should start from the very beginning to raise spiritually conscious, productive, caring children. If you are a childcare provider in any capacity, we recommend that you carefully ponder these 8 tips and expand upon them in your own life.

1. Demonstrate healthy, wholesome living, as an example for your child(ren). By your words, actions and thoughts, model for your children the kind of behavior that is acceptable and desirable. Create safe, nurturing environments as much as possible by direct, deliberate arrangements and by your example. Remember, children live what they learn.

2.   Do at least one family and spiritual activity together every day. Cook, eat, read, have conversations and/or say bedtime prayers together. When you are implementing family activity together, demonstrate the importance of family time by turning off the television, your cell phones, computer and/or radio and in general avoid interruptions.

3.   Give age appropriate chores, consequences and discipline. This will give your children a real sense of responsibility and fairness. For example, if you give a 3-year-old a time out and an 8-year-old a time out, the time spent "out" should be longer for the 8-year-old than the 3-year-old. (2-to-5-year-olds should receive 2-5 minute time-outs and 8-year-olds, about 5 minutes.) Make sure that your child is aware of the undesirable behavior that you are targeting. Keep in mind that you are building a healthy person.

4.   Help your children appreciate the importance of quiet or silent time. Spend quiet time reading, writing, meditating or drawing or reflecting on the day's events. Since we live in a culture that is constantly bombarded by sounds (many unnatural), stimulated and interrupted by phones, computers, television and other media, it is helpful to practice reducing external stimuli and teaching your children to be internal. This will assist with concentration, memory and appreciation of one's self as an important and thoughtful person in the circle of life. Allow at least 15 to 30 minutes a day. Even small children can learn to appreciate quietness. When they are older, this quiet time will help your children to focus for study, or for setting and implementing goals.

5. Seek to know and support your child(ren)'s talents and tendencies. Every child is unique and each child has his/her own different talent(s). Some children are musical or artistic, while others enjoy building objects or studying nature. Give them lessons, books, and/or materials, and an environment conducive to the growth of their talent gifts. Also, take note of some of the areas in which your child(ren) needs to grow or practice. Develop exercises, scenarios and consequences to assist with eliminating negative tendencies such as envy, greed, anger, unwillingness to share or bullying. At the same time, reinforce appropriate behavior and sincere efforts with praise. Be open to getting or refreshing your parenting skills through workshops, classes and parent groups.

Conscious parenting is intentional; what are the characteristics of the children you want to raise? While you may not and should not define your child's exact occupation or career, you can and should envision your child growing up with wholesome qualities and characteristics. You can envision your child being a kind, thoughtful and considerate person who contributes good things to the environment. From the very beginning, you can picture your child as a responsible, caring leader in whatever family and community he will eventually live in. Such intentions will frame how you interact with your children; how you educate them; how you expose them to culture and spirituality; how, when and what you feed them; and with whom you allow them to associate.

6. Teach your child early on about the importance of finances in general (tithing, saving, avoiding debt, the costs incurred in maintaining a house, interest rates) and the importance of utilizing God's resources in His service or in ways that are honest and conducive to healthy family and community growth.

7. Pay close attention to your children's diet. Many dedicated parents unknowingly feed their children foods that cause adverse effects, such as overly processed foods, fast foods, too many fried foods and not enough fresh fruits and vegetables. Often food additives contribute to hyperactivity, attention deficits and overly aggressive behavior in children. Do your homework: You will find so many researchers who have demonstrated time and again that some food colorings, artificial flavorings, pesticides and processed foods in general (including white sugar) are harmful to the health and well-being of our children. Pay attention to portion size and select natural, nutritious ingredients.

How you nourish your children will help them to establish habits that will benefit them their entire lives. Avoid processed food and meat products. Many of the meat sold in grocery stores today contain hormones and harmful chemicals. Conscientious people are choosing meatless diets because animals raised for meat production are frequently tortured and abused. Studies show that eating a balanced diet of fruits, vegetables, nuts and dairy is best for children and adults.

8. Teach your children to respect you, God, and other authorities in their lives. By respecting you, they will learn to respect elders, ministers, and teachers who are committed to their healthy learning and development. Help them to realize that when they respect appropriate authorities and elders in this way, they are actually respecting themselves. "Honor thy father and thy mother that thy days may be long upon the land which the Lord giveth thee." (Holy Bible, 4th Commandment)

8 Qualities of a Spiritual Warrior

A Native American elder described his own inner struggles this way: "Inside of me there are two dogs. One of the dogs is mean and evil. The other dog is good. The mean dog fights the good dog all the time." When asked which dog wins, he reflected for a moment and replied, "The one I feed the most." — Native American Proverb

As we follow spiritual laws, accomplish great things with self-discipline, and learn successful relationship skills, we often encounter great adversity. The Holy Bible speaks of these challenges in Mark: "We battle not against flesh and blood but against principalities and spiritual wickedness in high places."

In our own lives, these challenges may come in the form of personal or family struggles, financial difficulties or legal problems. The ancient Vedas describes 3 kinds of troubles or miseries in the material world:

1. Miseries inflicted by your own body or your own mind (headaches, emotional troubles, diseases);
2. Troubles imposed by other living entities (pests, enmity between neighbors); and
3. Miseries caused by supernatural influences or acts of nature (tornadoes, floods, famines, hurricanes).

When we understand that we are strong spiritual warriors, however, we tolerate or deal with these troubles with knowledge, hope and fortitude. Many of the world's great religious scriptures, the Bible, the Torah, the Qur'an and the Bhagavad-gita, declare that we must fight as instruments of God; thus, it is clear that we are on the battlefield in this world. The analogy of battle is frequently repeated in those scriptures and we are called to "put on the whole armor of God" (Bible) and to "give up such petty weakness and arise o chastiser of the enemy" (Bhagavad-gita). Additionally, the Qur'an informs us that the greatest jihad (fight) is the fight against (the lower) self.

Undoubtedly, those of us who aspire for higher consciousness and a principled, healthy lifestyle, recognize that we are spiritual warriors who must first triumph over the weaknesses and impure qualities within ourselves. The list below identifies the 8 primary qualities of a spiritual warrior.

1. **Truthful**: Lying destroys one of the four legs of real religion which are:

    ▪ Truthfulness
    ▪ Cleanliness
    ▪ Compassion
    ▪ Self-discipline (sometimes called austerity, includes charity)

Again, in the books of knowledge of the ancient Vedas, it is said that God loves the truthful soul. The Bible commands "Thou shall not bear false witness." Additionally, one of the foremost Eastern saints, Srila Rupa Goswami, emphasized that if one becomes accustomed to always speaking the truth, whatever one speaks, will eventually *be*(come) the truth. One major activity that destroys truthfulness is gambling. It promotes the idea that you can get a lot for a little or something for nothing. Gambling also encourages a kind of cheating mentality that diminishes our faith in God to provide what we need.

2. Clean: (inside and out) Cleanliness is not only next to Godliness, it is an inseparable part of Godly character. Undeniably, being clean externally by bathing, brushing, keeping your clothes, car and house clean is extremely important to a healthy, progressive life. Even more important, however is *internal* cleanliness. You do this by keeping your spiritual commitments or vows, by praying, by meditating, and by remembering the Creator as the Supreme Proprietor, the Supreme Enjoyer and the Best Friend of every living being, and by calling God's purifying names. "The most Beautiful Names belong to God, so call upon Him by Them" (Qur'an). "He who calls upon the name of the Lord shall be saved" (Bible).

3. Compassionate: Our tendency for showing mercy or kindness to other living beings is destroyed by intoxication — alcohol and drugs — and by consuming animal flesh (meat). When you eat meat or participate in the unnecessary killing of any life, particularly human and animals, then your sensitivity to the sufferings of other living beings is subtly eroded. The Bible says, "Thou shall not kill." In this divine commandment, there is no distinction given between killing an animal or killing a human being. By compassionately holding all life sacred, we honor God by fulfilling His desire. We should also prayerfully consider how our choices and violent behavior affect our lives, bringing some karmic results such as wars or more crime.

4. Self-disciplined: Often, we can always advise *others* how to behave better, but we generally experience a lot more difficulty seeing our own inadequacies. Exercising control in the things you do and avoiding the things that are harmful or detrimental to you and others requires strong self-discipline. For example, when you neglect to commit to a healthy lifestyle and to eat nutritious foods, you are more likely to develop health issues like heart disease, diabetes or high blood pressure. In this case, not only do you suffer physically, but your spirit and your character weakens. (Your greatest fight is the fight with your lower self.)

5. Humble: True humility is very empowering and comes in part when we realize that we are just an instrument for God's higher energies or, by default, His lower energies. The most advanced souls are the most humble. "One should be more tolerant than a tree, more humble than a blade of grass. In this way, one will continue to make spiritual progress and be near to God always" (Sri Siksastakam, Veda). If you choose the path of humility before a great big God, you will rarely have to be humiliated.

6. Surrendered: As a spiritual warrior, realize that you are the eternal servant of the Greatest Master. Acknowledge that God (the Ultimate Boss, the Supreme Owner and the Dearest Friend) nurtures your soul at all times. Though you may not always understand everything that is happening around you, or to you, you can take shelter in God's grace, knowing that you do your best to carry out His instructions as an honest, caring, God-conscious person. Always feeling protected and guided, you should open yourself to being a vehicle through which love, joy, peace and truth flow.

7. Eager to learn and to share knowledge: One of the most identifiable characteristics of the spiritual warrior is that you are always discovering things that uplift and nourish you and others, and you share the wisdom you've acquired.

8. Industrious: Spiritual warriors work hard to fulfill their responsibilities and achieve their goals. As a spiritual warrior, you choose to represent spiritual principles in your speech, your thoughts and your actions. By your steady and sincere willingness to work, you show your faith. "Faith without works is dead" (Bible).

Assess the ways in which you act as a spiritual warrior and make sure you "put on the whole armor of God" (Bible) every day. Sometimes if you feel that you do not possess a particular quality of a spiritual warrior, act in that way anyway, and gradually the quality will manifest more and more in your life.

8 Books to Read to Enhance Your Life

"Wisdom comes only when you stop looking for it and start living the life the Creator intended for you." –Hopi Proverb

Every year, thousands and thousands of books are published all over the world. From all the choices, how do we select the books that will educate, entertain and uplift us? Most of the books listed below have withstood the test of time and shine as exemplary literature to help us grow.

1. *Bhagavad-Gita As It Is*, translated by A. C. Bhaktivedanta Swami: A book of timeless Eastern wisdom that explores God, the variety of living entities, eternal time, material nature, karma, and how all of these interact with each other. Join the ranks of Emerson, Thoreau, Gandhi, George Harrison and others who have relished its profound spiritual knowledge. *Bhagavad-gita* is in the form of a dialogue between God and His devotee and takes place on a battlefield. Swami A. C. Bhaktivedanta Prabhupada is a scholar and advanced practitioner of Bhakti-yoga who presents these ancient teachings from the perspective of a self-realized soul.

2. *The Qur'an*: This Islamic holy book is fundamental to the spiritual understanding of millions around the world. Its basic theme is the relationship between God and His creatures while providing guidelines for human conduct, equitable economics and justice.

3. *The Holy Bible*: Containing timeless Christian parables of truth and spiritual knowledge, the Bible records the interaction of God with historical people and nations. It reveals the meaning of life and the responsibility of human beings to their Creator. Consisting of 66 books, it is the world's most translated book and the world's all-time best seller.

4. *Spiritual Warrior II (Transforming Lust into Love)* by Swami Krishnapada: "Today's world is suffering from an overdose of lust, while people everywhere are starving for love." In *Spiritual Warrior II*, Swami Krishnapada offers profound insight into the critical issues of the body, mind and spirit that touch us all. Tough questions are addressed: What is love? Where does lust come from? How can sexuality become a constructive force? How can we have better relationships?

5. *7 Habits of Highly Successful Families* by Stephen Covey: This book offers great guidelines on how to "build a beautiful family culture in a turbulent world." In it, you will find practical answers to many family challenges.

6. *Leadership for an Age of Higher Consciousness* by B.T. Swami: Addressing the leader within each of us, B.T. Swami shows us that the greatest leaders see themselves as servants first. Placing integrity and character before personal gain, they know how to tap into the help that is available from earthly *and* spiritual realms. The author explains the potency of "true servant leaders who are animated visionaries and who cultivate divine power to transform diverse individuals with scattered goals into communities with a unified, sacred mission." It gives powerful keys for effective and progressive leadership.

7. *Ethics for the New Millennium* by His Holiness the Dalai Lama: In this book, the Nobel Peace Laureate writes in simple direct prose about what he calls "certain basic facts of existence," such as the interdependence of all things, universal responsibility, care, compassion and how our happiness depends on positive ethical conduct.

8. *All I Really Need To Know I Learned In Kindergarten* by Robert Fulghum: In this charming book, Robert Fulghum presents simple profound truths that are quite practical in these oft-complicated times and demonstrates why "brevity is indeed the soul of wit." If adults followed these "childish" rules, such as "clean up your mess," share, and balance work with play, the world would be a truly gentler, kinder and friendlier place.

Take the time to read these books, over time if you will, and you will be blessed with benefits that are worth far more than the time you invested. For these books feed your mind and your soul, and isn't it "written that man shall not live by bread alone"?

About the Author

Krsnanandini Devi Dasi is a minister, Certified Family Life
Educator (CFLE), wife, and mother of ten. As Co-Director of
the Dasi-Ziyad Family Institute, she has worked with
hundreds of individuals and couples, providing them with
Healthy Relationship Education; and has co-presented and
created scores of relationship, family and youth character
building workshops, magazine articles, curricula and
courses such as the S.E.L.F (Singles Evaluating Life and
Family) Healthy Relationship course, the Young Pioneer
Project, Parenting for the 21st Century, and more.

Raised in a Christian family, she has studied Islam,
Mormonism and Hinduism to appreciate the underlying
unity in all the world's religions. She was initiated in the
ancient Vaisnava spiritual culture in 1972 and has been a
practitioner of Bhakti-yoga (the yoga of devotion to God)
since that time. Ms. Dasi is dedicated to being an instrument
of God's joy, peace and love.

She resides with her husband and children in Cleveland,
Ohio.

www.ingramcontent.com/pod-product-compliance
Lightning Source LLC
Chambersburg PA
CBHW021921040426
42448CB00007B/862